SELF-CARE FOR EVERY DAY JOURNAL

Simple Tips and Guided Exercises to Help You Feel Your Best

vie

SELF-CARE FOR EVERY DAY JOURNAL

This fully updated and revised edition copyright © Octopus Publishing Group Limited, 2026
First published as *Self-Care for Every Day* in 2023

All rights reserved.

Text by Victoria Maw, updated and revised by Holly Brook-Piper

No part of this book may be reproduced by any means, nor transmitted, nor translated into a machine language, without the written permission of the publishers.

Condition of Sale
This book is sold subject to the condition that it shall not, by way of trade or otherwise, be lent, resold, hired out or otherwise circulated in any form of binding or cover other than that in which it is published and without a similar condition including this condition being imposed on the subsequent purchaser.

An Hachette UK Company
www.hachette.co.uk

Vie Books, an imprint of Summersdale Publishers
Part of Octopus Publishing Group Limited
Carmelite House
50 Victoria Embankment
LONDON
EC4Y 0DZ
UK

This FSC® label means that materials and other controlled sources used for the product have been responsibly sourced

www.summersdale.com

The authorized representative in the EEA is Hachette Ireland, 8 Castlecourt Centre, Dublin 15, D15 XTP3, Ireland (email: info@hbgi.ie)

Printed and bound in China

ISBN: 978-1-83799-136-5
eISBN: 978-1-83799-842-5

Substantial discounts on bulk quantities of Summersdale books are available to corporations, professional associations and other organizations. For details contact general enquiries: telephone: +44 (0) 1243 771107 or email: enquiries@summersdale.com.

This journal belongs to:

Date of birth:

Date:

How I feel before embarking on this journey:

Completion date:

How I feel now I have completed this journey:

INTRODUCTION

Self-care can seem like a big task. You might think that it costs lots of money, or that it takes hours, but it simply means taking care of yourself through small acts of kindness. And it's not just important – it's vital. When we don't take care of ourselves, we feel physically and emotionally depleted.

You may find it difficult to make time to look after yourself, as many of us do, but with the help of this journal, you can introduce self-care practices into your everyday life.

HOW TO USE THIS JOURNAL

Journalling is most effective when you do it regularly, so put aside a few moments every day to work through the prompts on the following pages. By making it a habit, you will discover that self-care becomes a way of life instead of something you struggle to make time for.

Try to include as much detail in your answers as you can because this will provide greater insight into your thoughts and feelings. Don't let anything hold you back – there is no right or wrong way to write in this journal. It is yours and yours alone, so be honest with yourself and try to not censor your writing.

LISTEN IN

Many of us are good at understanding the needs of our family and friends. But when it comes to understanding our own needs – like nourishing our bodies or taking care of our emotional needs – we can feel clueless. The secret is to listen a little harder.

Real self-care is about noticing what you need and making time for it. This might involve doing something you love or something you've always wanted to do, but it can also be about the *not* doing – resting or choosing to prioritize yourself. Make time to listen to your body and emotions and create some mental space so you can figure out what it is that you really need right now. Dive deep and don't be afraid. Self-care can be magical! We all deserve to feel taken care of – it is the greatest kindness we can offer ourselves.

Use the space below to answer the following questions:

What does self-care mean to you?

What do you want to achieve through practising regular self-care?

How often would you like to practise self-care? Set a self-care aim – even if it's 5 minutes a day.

What emotional and physical needs would you like to focus on during this self-care journey?

Listening to what your body and mind need is a form of self-care. You can do this by focusing on activities that replenish your energy.

This kind of nurturing can differ for each person, from taking a bubble bath to going out for a cup of coffee or even dancing to your own tunes at home.

List five things you think could help nurture your soul and body.

> JUST WHEN YOU FEEL YOU HAVE NO TIME TO RELAX, KNOW THAT THIS IS THE MOMENT YOU MOST NEED TO MAKE TIME TO RELAX.
>
> Matt Haig

TALK TO YOURSELF KINDLY

While we often speak to our friends with compassion, supporting their successes and cheering them up when they feel down, we do not always treat ourselves in the same way. Negative self-talk can have a significant effect on your self-image. Instead, look in the mirror and try saying something kind to yourself. While it may feel awkward at first, persevere – the more you practise, the more natural it will feel.

- Remind yourself of when you last did something thoughtful for somebody.
- Think back to the last time you smiled at a stranger.
- Tell yourself about something you are good at.
- Recall someone who is happy to see you every day.

Label each petal with something that you love about yourself.

Write a list of four things you are good at. This could also include your achievements.

1. ....
2. ....
3. ....
4. ....

Now describe how it feels to acknowledge what makes you great!

....
....
....
....

Next time you hear your negative inner voice, don't pay attention to it – come back to this page for an instant boost.

Use this space to write your own thoughts.

SELF-CARE IS SO
MUCH MORE THAN
A BEAUTY REGIMEN
OR AN EXTERNAL
THING YOU DO.

Carrie-Anne Moss

Journal into the Deep

Journalling is, put simply, the act of writing down your thoughts and feelings. It can be a fantastic outlet if you are feeling anxious or stressed, as well as a place to plan what you need to do each day.

There are many different ways to approach journalling, whether it is recounting your day, listing the things you are grateful for or responding to journalling prompts. But sometimes a structure can be limiting. In her popular book *The Artist's Way*, Julia Cameron describes a technique called "Morning Pages". This process involves producing three pages of longhand stream of consciousness every morning. To do this, you write your thoughts and feelings as they come, not worrying whether they make sense, or about correct spelling or grammar. Why not have a go? Write about whatever you want – your day, the weather, your feelings, the shopping list. Once you clear out the noise – the admin and the to-do lists – you might just find ideas and inspiration hiding beneath.

Practise freewriting below and on the following pages. Don't hold back or worry about spelling and handwriting; instead just take the opportunity to clear your mind. Try doing this exercise every day for a week. Here are some prompts to get you started:

- What are you doing right now?
- How are you feeling?
- What has made you smile this week?

Talking to yourself kindly can be challenging. But a part of self-care for every day includes letting your inner voice be kind to you. Replace hurtful or critical feelings with positivity and encouragement to create a nurturing environment.

Try writing down 10 sentences of positive self-talk and then say them out loud to yourself while standing in front of a mirror.

1.
2.
3.
4.
5.
6.
7.
8.
9.
10.

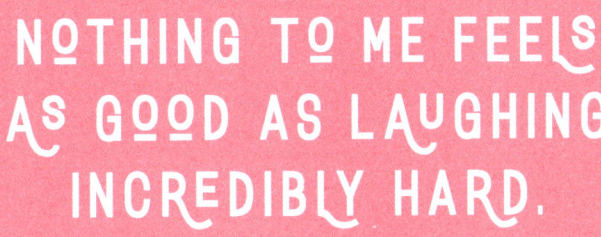

NOTHING TO ME FEELS
AS GOOD AS LAUGHING
INCREDIBLY HARD.

Steve Carell

TAKE YOURSELF ON A DATE

Celebrate self-love by taking yourself out! How do you enjoy spending your time when it is just you? If you could plan a lovely day for yourself, what would you do? Perhaps you would enjoy lunch in a new café with a good book, or visit that exhibition or watch that movie you've been wanting to see.

Your plans don't have to cost much. In fact, there are many ways to treat yourself for free! You could pack a rucksack and take yourself on a hike or explore a new part of town, or you could spend the day lying in a park and listening to music.

See this "date" as a chance to enjoy your own company and to follow your whims and desires. It might be the first time in a long while that you have put your needs before anybody else's.

What do you want to get out of your date?

For example, do you want it to be stimulating or fun, or would you rather use the time to relax?

What would your ideal solo date involve?

Plan your perfect day of self-care activities:

Morning:
Afternoon:
Evening:

Use this space to write your own thoughts.

Find Your Exercise

Love it or lump it, the science is clear: exercise is good for us, and it is as vital for our mental health as it is for our physical health.

There are many ways to move, so there's no point forcing yourself to do a type of exercise that you dislike. There will always be people who love running, but if you don't enjoy it, try something different. If you are someone who loves connecting with nature, try taking your exercise outdoors. If you are a sociable person, a group dance class or joining your local tennis club might be more your thing.

Be realistic and approach exercise with an open mind until you find the activity that works for you.

Write a list of the types of exercise that you enjoy or would like to try.

- ....
- ....
- ....
- ....

- ....
- ....
- ....
- ....

Using the planner below, pick some types of exercise from the list above and then add them to your weekly routine. Every time you complete an exercise, give it a tick and a rating from 1 to 10 for enjoyment, 10 being the most enjoyable.

Day	Exercise	✓	Rating 1–10
Mon			
Tue			
Wed			
Thurs			
Fri			
Sat			
Sun			

We know that exercise is good for our physical and mental well-being. Still, people often find it challenging to take the first step. Sometimes, these barriers can be mental rather than physical, such as concerns about our appearance or what others might think.

It's best to deal with your mental barriers first. Listing them out can make it easier to talk about them with family and friends and find ways to resolve them yourself.

Use the space on this page to write down your worries.

....
....
....
....
....
....
....
....
....
....

TRAVEL AND
CHANGE OF PLACE
IMPART NEW VIGOUR
TO THE MIND.

Seneca

BELLY BREATHING

Breathing into your belly has all sorts of amazing benefits. It encourages better oxygen flow around the body, reduces stress levels and relaxes the nervous system. And the best part: the results are instantaneous.

So, how do you do it? Start by getting really comfortable, either by sitting or lying down. Place both hands on your belly, relax your shoulders and try to release any tension from your jaw. Inhale through your nose for a count of five, breathing into your abdomen and feeling it expand like a balloon under your hands. As you exhale through your mouth, allow every part of your body to soften and relax completely. Inhale and expand, then exhale and soften. Practise this process several times and observe how you feel afterwards.

Next time you're feeling stressed, notice what part of your body you are breathing from. If it's right up in your chest, find somewhere to sit comfortably and try belly breathing to help you find your calm.

Take some time out to try the breathing exercise on the opposite page. Answer the following questions about how these breathing exercises made you feel before, during and after doing them.

1. How do you feel before practising the breathing exercise?

....

....

....

2. How did you feel during the belly breathing?

....

....

....

3. How do you feel after completing the exercise? Describe the effects belly breathing had on your mind and body.

....

....

....

Use this space to write your own thoughts.

> TO LOVE ONESELF IS THE BEGINNING OF A LIFELONG ROMANCE.
>
> Oscar Wilde

REACH OUT TO A FRIEND

We all have people in our lives whose company we thrive upon. Individuals who support us and make us feel good about ourselves are integral to our wellness and happiness, boosting our self-confidence, providing a sense of belonging and offering support in times of need. Yet sometimes it can be easy to go weeks (or even months) without connecting.

Reaching out to those most important in our lives can remind us that we are lucky to have such friendship and love, and also gives us an opportunity to thank them for it. Try not to let friendships take a back seat – instead, make them a priority. So, make that call, set up a coffee date or plan a trip with someone important to you. Taking this leap can have a significant impact on your emotional well-being, as well as that of the person you have reached out to. It's a win–win!

Write a list of any friends or family you would like to reconnect with. When you feel ready, give them a call or send them a message.

👤

👤

👤

👤

👤

👤

Come up with some activities you could enjoy together. It might be as simple as a walk in the park, or something more extravagant, such as a big night out.

-
-
-
-
-
-

Reaching out to your friends or family after not speaking to them for a long time can feel daunting. Sometimes, it's easier to text, but other times, you find yourself postponing a meet-up further away. In such cases, it's essential to recognize that there could be deep-rooted issues as to why you resist reaching out to them.

Use the safe space below to think about what is mentally stopping you from contacting them.

Do not anticipate trouble or worry about what may never happen. Keep in the sunlight.

Benjamin Franklin

Take Your Tea Outside

Chances are, you start your day with a cup of tea or coffee. But what do you do once you've made your drink? Instead of rushing to get on with your work or chores, drinking on the go, take a few minutes to open a window or step outside and feel the fresh air and (if you're lucky) the sun on your face.

Be present for a moment. Take a few deep breaths and pay attention to the sounds outside – from birds, to chatter, to traffic. It can be easy to gulp down a coffee without noticing the taste or the temperature, so try to savour the small pleasure of a hot drink on a new day.

We so often jump straight into our day without remembering to check in on ourselves. Just taking these extra moments can be a valuable way to start the morning – by doing so, you will feel more present and connected to yourself.

Take 10 minutes at the beginning of your day to appreciate the moment. Notice each of your five senses: sight, touch, hearing, smell and taste.

What can you see, feel, hear, smell and taste in this moment?

How does it feel to be more present and connected?

In the space below, consider the different points in your day when you could take a 5-minute break to check in with yourself.

Use this space to write your own thoughts.

TAKING CARE OF MYSELF BRINGS ME HAPPINESS

MICRO-TIDYING

Mess in your home can leave you feeling stressed and anxious, and you may not feel comfortable enough to relax there. When clutter overwhelms your space, it might seem impossible to know where to start, or that you will ever have the time or energy to sort everything out.

A micro-tidy means choosing just one thing – a drawer, a shelf, a corner of the kitchen – to clean and organize. Clear the space, clean the surface and then put things back neatly, setting aside anything you no longer need. If items are no longer being used, it's probably time to get rid of them. Unwanted items can be sold on the internet, donated or recycled.

By taking these small steps, you can start to relieve any anxiety caused by clutter, making your home somewhere you enjoy spending time.

Use the table below to help you plan your micro-tidying. Select one area of your home to organize each day. Every time you complete your task, give it a tick.

	Area to be decluttered	✓
Mon		
Tue		
Wed		
Thurs		
Fri		
Sat		
Sun		

How did the process of decluttering make you feel?

....

....

....

....

....

....

Micro-tidying sounds like a neat idea, but where to start? Knowing how to begin and where to tidy up your space can be overwhelming. Start by thinking which part of your room or house is most essential in your daily life.

List such areas from high to low priority, and you will know where to begin!

> REST AND SELF-CARE ARE SO IMPORTANT... YOU CANNOT SERVE FROM AN EMPTY VESSEL.
>
> Eleanor Brownn

WALK WITH AWARENESS

Are you guilty of walking from A to B without noticing anything around you? Perhaps you walk and talk on your phone at the same time or listen to music or podcasts. While this can feel efficient, there are huge mental benefits to be found from simply observing your surroundings.

Next time you need to go out, try engaging all your senses as you take in your environment. What can you see and hear? What is new in your neighbourhood? What seasonal changes have happened since you last walked this route? Really take notice of all the details – you will be surprised by how much you miss when you are preoccupied with other things. The act of noticing sights, sounds and smells is a form of meditation, keeping you absolutely in the moment and helping to calm a busy mind.

Next time you go for a walk, take the opportunity to fully observe your surroundings. When you get back, write down:

Five things you saw:
1.
2.
3.
4.
5.

Four things you felt:
1.
2.
3.
4.

Three things you heard:
1.
2.
3.

Two things you smelled:
1.
2.

One thing you tasted:
1.

How did taking notice of your surroundings change your experience?

Use this space to write your own thoughts.

SELF-LOVE HAS VERY LITTLE TO DO WITH HOW YOU FEEL ABOUT YOUR OUTER SELF. IT'S ABOUT ACCEPTING ALL OF YOURSELF.

Tyra Banks

SPENDING AUDIT

This one might not sound like much fun, but it's often the jobs we put off that stress us out the most. Spending some time reviewing your outgoings is a way to take control of your finances. This can be especially helpful if you're trying to save up for something and is often really empowering.

Make a warm drink, sit down with a spreadsheet or a notebook, and get to grips with it all. List all your expenses, then note down all the things you are saving up for. Remember to include all the one-off costs as well as the regular ones. This is one of those jobs that takes a bit of time, but the hardest part is actually deciding to get on with it. Once you've finished and have the facts to hand, you may feel a sense of relief. Whatever happens, you'll be armed with the knowledge to take the next steps.

Use the table below to get a basic overview of your spending habits.

Expense	Amount	Regular or one-off?

What are you currently saving up for? Can you see anywhere you can cut back to help you achieve this faster?

Trying to cut back on expenses can seem like a lot of work. One way to start making changes is to look at the recurring expenses you might have, such as paying for a streaming service you don't watch anymore.

Please use the space below to list all your recurring expenses and see if you can find things to cut back on.

....

....

....

....

....

....

....

....

....

....

....

DON'T BE AFRAID.
BE FOCUSED.
BE DETERMINED.
BE HOPEFUL.
BE EMPOWERED.

Michelle Obama

Make an Inspiration Board

It feels good to be reminded of the things we love or that support our creativity, and while we could simply write them down, a pictorial reminder can be even more powerful. One way to do this is to make a board of inspiring words and images to keep on a desk or pin up in the kitchen. There are no rules, so feel free to be as creative as you like!

Start with a pin board or a square of cardboard that you could cover in fabric, or perhaps use washi tape to stick things directly on a wall. Gather up postcards, magazine cut-outs or photographs that you like and write out inspiring quotes from people you admire. You could even add notes from family and friends. Make your inspiration board a little piece of you and the things you love.

Use this page to plan your inspiration board. Add anything that makes you smile or inspires you. Come back to this page and add more ideas.

Use this space to write your own thoughts.

I WILL MAKE SELF-CARE A PRIORITY

LIMIT NEWS CONSUMPTION

Do you find yourself glued to the newsfeed on your phone? Doomscrolling – compulsively scrolling through bad news on social media – can have a significant negative impact on your mental health. Spending hours consuming news can be draining, and can leave us feeling helpless and anxious. Over time, this can take its toll.

It can be a good idea to set a time limit for how long you spend reading the news. To counteract some of the negative news, also try to look at "good news" websites and magazines to remind yourself that, although the world can be a challenging place, it is also full of acts of kindness and generosity.

Find some good news stories and document them in the space below. Revisit this page whenever you feel the need for a positivity boost.

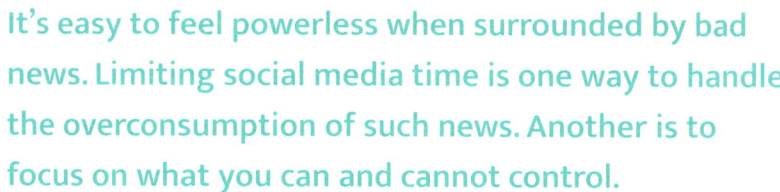

It's easy to feel powerless when surrounded by bad news. Limiting social media time is one way to handle the overconsumption of such news. Another is to focus on what you can and cannot control.

Sometimes, talking about it with your friends or family might help. Avoid keeping things to yourself.

Use this space to list things you can do to help a cause, either by spreading awareness or through monetary means.

_____

_____

_____

_____

_____

_____

_____

_____

_____

_____

I THINK IT'S JUST AS IMPORTANT WHAT YOU SAY NO TO AS WHAT YOU SAY YES TO.

Sandra Oh

STAY HYDRATED

Water is vital for good health and yet lots of us don't drink enough of it. Even when we become slightly dehydrated, the effects are obvious: poor concentration, headaches, dizziness and lethargy.

Make a promise to yourself to prioritize your hydration – one of the most basic but important forms of self-care. Remember to bring your water bottle with you, swap out caffeinated drinks for herbal teas, or infuse a jug of water with cucumber, lemon, celery or mint – whatever it takes to make sure you get around two litres, or six to eight glasses, of water into your system each day.

Monitor how many glasses of water you have every day for a week using the tracker below. Fill in one droplet for every glass that you drink. If after the first two or three days you notice that you aren't drinking enough, prioritize drinking more for the rest of the week.

Day								
Mon	○	○	○	○	○	○	○	○
Tue	○	○	○	○	○	○	○	○
Wed	○	○	○	○	○	○	○	○
Thurs	○	○	○	○	○	○	○	○
Fri	○	○	○	○	○	○	○	○
Sat	○	○	○	○	○	○	○	○
Sun	○	○	○	○	○	○	○	○

At the end of the week, document how staying hydrated has benefitted your mental and physical health.

Use this space to write your own thoughts.

> KEEP GOOD COMPANY,
> READ GOOD BOOKS,
> LOVE GOOD THINGS AND
> CULTIVATE SOUL AND
> BODY AS FAITHFULLY
> AS YOU CAN.
>
> Louisa May Alcott

Plant a Seed

Gardening is a fantastic self-care practice for anyone, no matter your age. Have you ever witnessed the joy of a toddler planting a tiny sunflower seed and watching it transform into a giant flower? The process of watching seeds grow can seem like magic, but perhaps the greatest pleasure comes from the fact that it takes only a short while to receive the fruits of your labour. Why not try planting your own seeds, or creating a mini herb garden? Whether it's flowers to decorate your home or vegetables to nourish your body, all it takes is a packet of seeds, a sunny windowsill and a little patience. So, what are you waiting for? Plant a seed to grow a self-care habit!

What types of plants would you like to grow?

- ....
- ....
- ....
- ....
- ....
- ....

Write a list of what you will need to get started.

- ....
- ....
- ....
- ....
- ....
- ....

After you have planted your seeds, use the space below to document their transformation from seed to plant.

....

....

....

....

Give yourself some positive vibes with a daily dose of sunshine. According to research, getting out into the morning sunshine helps your internal clock balance, so that you can get a good night's sleep. It also helps increase levels of serotonin – the "happy hormone" – in the brain.

Even if it's for 10 minutes, try going out each morning for 10 days and see how you feel about this.

Use the space below to write down your observations.

SELF-CARE IS NEVER SELFISH, BUT IT MAY FEEL THAT WAY WHEN YOU LIVE A FRENZIED LIFE.

Arthur P. Ciaramicoli

LET IT GO

We all carry emotional baggage with us. We hold on to old arguments, hurtful words, things left unsaid or behaviours we regret, and sometimes holding on to this burden can prevent us from moving forwards with our lives.

Take a moment to identify the source of your negative emotions. Recognizing the cause of these feelings can help you to manage them. What more could be possible if you decided to release whatever you are holding on to, or if you forgave yourself for a mistake? The best thing you can do is learn from the past and then let it go.

In the space below, write down anything that you feel is stopping you from moving forwards with your life. When you are finished, reread each experience and consider what more would be possible if you let go of the hurt. When you are ready to let them go, cross out each one and move on.

-
-
-
-
-
-
-
-

What have you learned from letting go of these negative experiences?

Use this space to write your own thoughts.

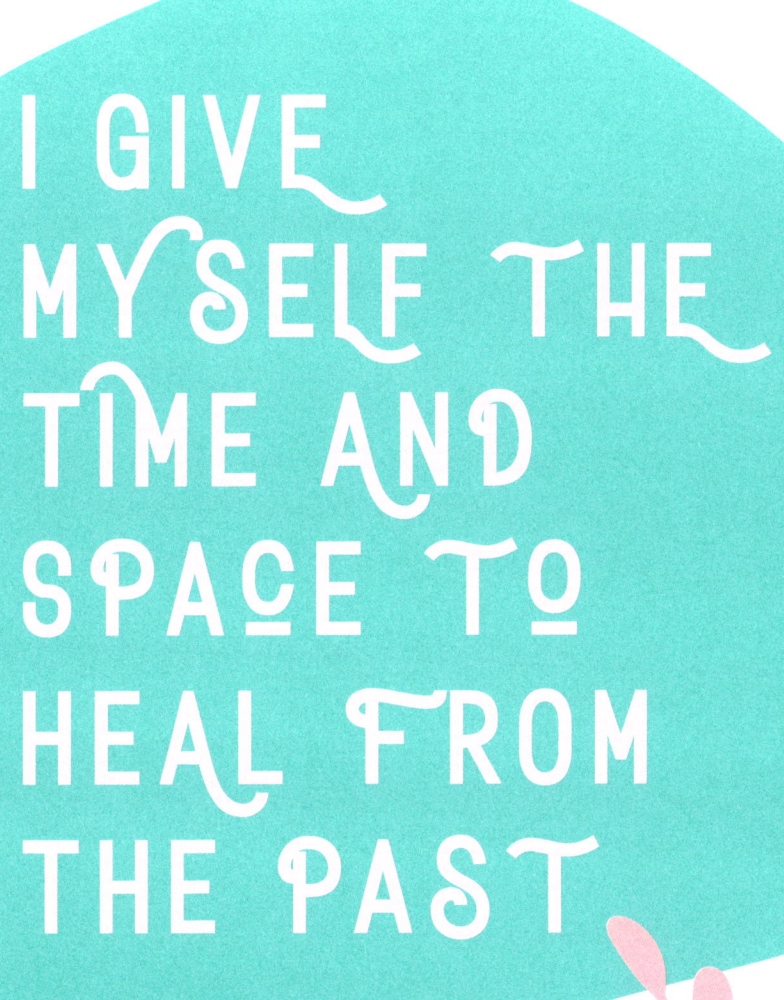

HAVE AN APP CLEAR-OUT

Smartphone technology means that we are more distracted than ever. Every day we are interrupted by alerts: our phones vibrate with emails during mealtimes and group chats fill our screens with messages. It can be exhausting to keep up, and it's no wonder that many of us struggle to concentrate when our attention is constantly being pulled in different directions.

Try to notice how these distractions make you feel. When your smartphone alerts you to yet another notification, ask yourself: who or what is losing out on your attention? Next time you have a few minutes spare, try to do an audit of your phone. Could you delete a few apps, or exit group chats that no longer serve you? You could also consider setting time limits on the apps you would like to continue using. Making a few changes will allow you to reclaim a little time and focus on the things that really matter to you.

What are your reasons for wanting to cut down on screen time?

- ....

- ....

- ....

Note down any apps on your phone that you feel distract you, and those which you would like to cut down on.

....

....

In the space below, set yourself a time limit for using your phone.

....

Write a list of the things you want to spend your time doing instead.

- ....

- ....

- ....

- ....

When trying to take a break from work, the general human tendency is to jump on your phone to scroll on social media or start watching something on a streaming platform. While this is good for entertainment, it prevents your brain from taking a break and so can have a negative impact on your mental well-being.

Note down how many times you used your phone without taking a break, and analyze how you can cut back on screen time and be present in the moment.

....

....

....

....

....

....

....

....

....

....

> CARVE OUT AND CLAIM THE TIME TO CARE FOR YOURSELF AND KINDLE YOUR OWN FIRE.
>
> Amy Ippoliti

Make a Wish

It might sound corny, but it can feel good to make a wish! We all have hopes, dreams and aspirations, and wishing for something can help us realize it. Achieving an aspiration is also a great way to boost your self-esteem.

While you might not believe in the art of manifestation, just writing down a wish or speaking it aloud can take you one step closer to achieving it. Think of something you would like to accomplish and write it down on a piece of paper. Keep it inside your bag as a reminder of your goal and to keep you on track. Have some self-belief and know that you are deserving of your wishes coming true.

If you could make one wish come true, what would it be?

What does this wish mean to you?

....

....

How would your life improve if this wish were to come true?

....

....

What steps can you take to help this wish come to fruition?

....

....

Use this space to write your own thoughts.

TALK TO YOURSELF
LIKE YOU WOULD TO
SOMEONE YOU LOVE.

Brené Brown

USE A MANTRA

In Eastern spiritual practices, a "mantra" is a sacred word that is thought to have a special power when repeated aloud. Using a mantra as part of your meditation practice can help to focus the mind, silence inner chatter and calm the nervous system.

Mantras were traditionally Sanskrit words, such as "om" (thought to be the sound of the universe) and "soham" (which translates to "I am that"). In modern times, we can also use words or short phrases that are meaningful and affirming to us, such as "I am enough", "I can do it", "keep breathing" or something else totally personal to you. Find a phrase that resonates with you and say it to yourself as part of your meditation practice. Try this for a few minutes each day and notice how your mantra makes you feel.

Come up with some of your own mantras to help focus your mind.

- ....
- ....
- ....
- ....
- ....
- ....
- ....
- ....

Repeat your mantras to yourself daily for a week. When the week is up, use the space below to record how this form of self-care has benefitted you.

....
....
....
....
....

You'll be surprised to know what a wonder a good shower is to your mental health. An "everything shower" is a good self-care activity, where you can do haircare and skincare routines, including exfoliating, hair masks, shaving, serums, face masks and body oil. Feel free to use any of your favourite products that make you happy and feel good about yourself.

Use this space to note down all the products you'll need for this shower. Do this once a week and write down how it makes you feel.

FOLLOW YOUR INSTINCTS. THIS IS WHERE TRUE WISDOM MANIFESTS ITSELF.

Oprah Winfrey

Doodling for Relaxation

Doodling can be incredibly soothing and the joy of drawing freely in particular is that you have no plan whatsoever. It's mark making just for the sake of it – and one of the great things about it is that there is no right or wrong!

Grab whatever paper you've got to hand – an envelope, leaflet or this journal will do – and just start drawing. If you need a starting point, pick a shape, such as a circle, a heart or spiral, and work outwards from there. Find your calm as you let your thoughts wander and embrace the therapeutic effects that doodling can have on your mind and body. Be playful, experimental and free, and see where it takes you!

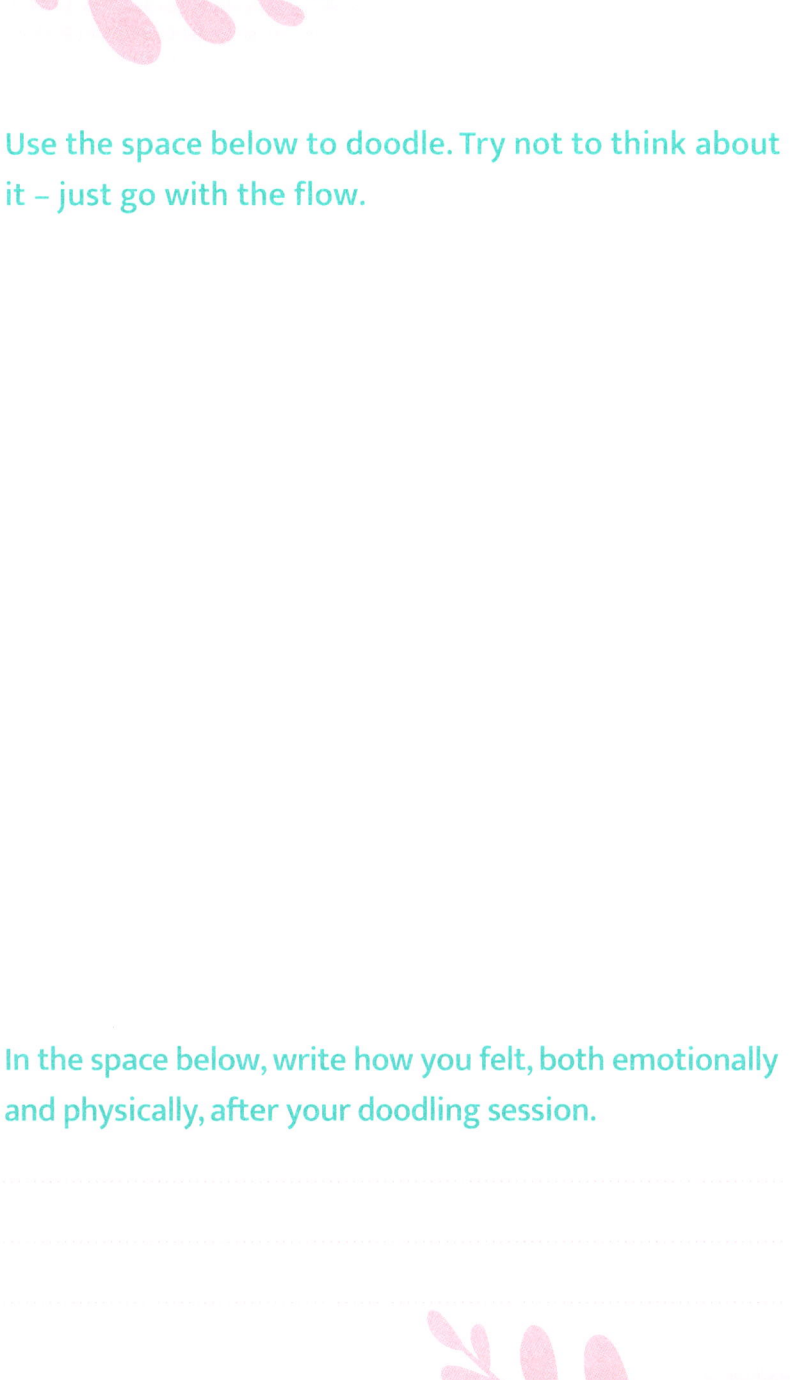

Use the space below to doodle. Try not to think about it – just go with the flow.

In the space below, write how you felt, both emotionally and physically, after your doodling session.

Use this space to write your own thoughts.

I APPRECIATE MY BODY AND EVERYTHING IT DOES FOR ME

FIND YOUR COMMUNITY

Isolation and loneliness can be a huge problem, and not just for the elderly – it can strike at any stage of life. As humans, we are social beings who thrive in communities, especially those where we meet like-minded individuals as well as people from different walks of life who bring their own experiences and advice to the room.

If you feel that you lack a community, remember that it can be found in many different places. Some people discover theirs by following their spirituality, whether that's through their religion or an activity like yoga or meditation. If this isn't for you, think about your interests and seek out people who share them. Could you join a choir or a book club, for example? You could also consider what skills you have to contribute to your local community. Could you get involved with a charity or help organize an event in your neighbourhood? Your people are out there – it's just a case of finding them.

What interests do you have that you would like to share with others?

- ....
- ....
- ....
- ....
- ....
- ....

What skills do you have to contribute to your local community? For example, if you are good at baking, you could be a great asset for a fundraiser.

....

....

....

Research local clubs or events in your area and use the space below to write down any important findings. It could be the start of something new for you.

....

....

....

It's easier to feel lonely when you're settled far away from your friends and family. In such cases, you can spiral down the path of overthinking. It can be difficult to plan outings, but you could try doing something online with your friends. It can either be playing games while chatting through headphones or simply watching a movie on a shared platform.

Use this space to write down a list of things you would like to do with your friends online and see how that makes you feel.

BE HEALTHY AND TAKE CARE OF YOURSELF, BUT BE HAPPY WITH THE BEAUTIFUL THINGS THAT MAKE YOU, YOU.

Beyoncé

LISTEN TO A PODCAST

In a busy, fast-paced world it can be hard to find the time to devote to learning something new, but thanks to the accessibility of podcasts, you can tune in to something new while you are on the go. Whether your passions lie in writing, gardening, activism, Pilates or something else entirely, there's a podcast for you.

The wonderful thing about a podcast is that you can listen pretty much anywhere, even when you are doing something less enjoyable, such as commuting, washing-up or cleaning the bathroom. Search by topic or person, and you might be amazed by what you find – perhaps an inspiring conversation or some advice and encouragement to feed the soul.

What types of subjects interest you the most?

- ....
- ....
- ....
- ....
- ....
- ....

Spend some time researching podcasts and list those that you would like to listen to. Next time you find yourself doomscrolling, why not try out one of the podcasts you've made a note of instead?

- ....
- ....
- ....

Note down the times or places that would be best suited to you to listen to your chosen podcasts.

- ....
- ....
- ....

Use this space to write your own thoughts.

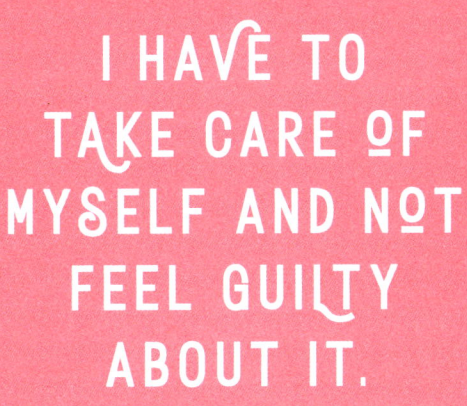

"I have to take care of myself and not feel guilty about it."

Selena Gomez

STARGAZING FOR WELL-BEING

On a clear night when the stars are out, it can feel pretty magical to gaze up and wonder at the magnitude of the sky. Just pondering the stars and planets above is enough to make us feel like part of a vast, complicated universe. Sometimes we can feel detached from the world around us, but an evening spent under the stars might be enough to remind us that we are all part of the same universe, connected to each other and to the world around us. It is also a beautiful way to enjoy the calming powers of the great outdoors.

On a clear night, take 5 minutes to relax and watch the night sky. In the space below, sketch out any constellations you can see. Around the outside, write as many adjectives as possible that describe the experience.

Walking with awareness, also known as mindful walking, is when you pay attention to your surroundings and bodily sensations as you are walking. An essential part is leaving behind your earphones or headphones. You'll be surprised to learn how much of a difference this process can make in helping you achieve your goal of being aware of your surroundings.

Note how impactful your experience was when using your earphones vs when not using them while walking outside.

....

....

....

....

....

....

....

....

....

....

....

WHOEVER IS HAPPY
WILL MAKE OTHERS
HAPPY TOO.

Anne Frank

The Power of Sharing

The phrase "sharing is caring" is often directed at young children, but in a world where wastage is a huge problem, it could be better applied to adults. Sharing can help us look after the planet and those around us while also encouraging sustainability.

There are many sharing websites available, such as The Freecycle Network and Sharebay, where you can find any items you need and in turn share your own unused belongings. Consider borrowing an outfit for a party rather than buying a new one, or lending the garden and electrical equipment you have in the shed to someone who could make good use of it. Sharing your possessions in your local community could also help you to connect with those around you.

Can you think of a time when you shared something with someone? In the space below, describe how this experience made you feel.

....

....

....

Is there anything you own that could be shared to benefit others in your local community?

- ....
- ....
- ....
- ....

Look up free sharing sites online and write your findings in the space below. Next time you need something, rather than buying it, come back to this page to remind you where you could borrow it instead.

- ....
- ....
- ....
- ....
- ....
- ....

Use this space to write your own thoughts.

I AM HAPPY BEING ME

CHECK IN WITH YOURSELF

It is normal to have a weekly meeting to check in with your team at work, but have you ever thought about having a check-in with yourself? Could you improve your week by examining the previous one, celebrating your triumphs or reminding yourself of the things you might like to approach differently?

A personal check-in could take whatever form you like. It could be helpful to look holistically at all areas of your life, whether that's your relationships, fitness or mental health, or you could set yourself a target for the week ahead. You could also re-examine goals, set to-do lists or simply look through all the things you have achieved and give yourself a pat on the back. Reward your hard work by scheduling in a treat, like a lunchtime walk or a coffee with a friend.

At the beginning of each week, set aside some time to check in on yourself and ask the following questions:

How am I feeling about the week ahead?

Week 1

Week 2

Week 3

What do I need to achieve this week?

Week 1

Week 2

Week 3

Could any areas of my life be improved?

Week 1

Week 2

Week 3

How could I do this?

Week 1

Week 2

Week 3

A mix of green and blue environments can do wonders for our health. This means going to as many green places as possible, such as a park, and blue spaces like the seaside. Breathing in the fresh air at these places helps reduce stress and build stronger immunity while encouraging a healthy lifestyle.

Look into five green and blue places where you can breathe fresh air. Use this space to write down where and when you would like to go.

....

....

....

....

....

....

....

....

....

> HOW WE CARE FOR OURSELVES GIVES OUR BRAIN MESSAGES THAT SHAPE OUR SELF-WORTH, SO WE MUST CARE FOR OURSELVES IN EVERY WAY, EVERY DAY.
>
> Sam Owen

Write a Thank-You Note

A handwritten thank-you note is a joy to receive – it makes us feel so much more special than when we receive a text or an email. But it can feel as good to do the thanking as it does to be thanked!

Who could you write a thank-you note to? It doesn't need to be for anything grand, perhaps just the cup of coffee someone invited you around for or the garden produce you were given by a neighbour. Enjoy writing your note on beautiful paper or a postcard while you remember the person and occasion for which you are thankful. It comes at very little cost and has the power to make the recipient feel appreciated. What's more, you will both get a mood boost!

Use the space below to draft a thank-you note to someone for something you are grateful for.

To

Use this space to write your own thoughts.

SELF-COMPASSION
IS SIMPLY GIVING
THE SAME KINDNESS
TO OURSELVES
THAT WE WOULD
GIVE TO OTHERS.

Christopher Germer

Buy Yourself a Beauty Treat

While it's true that there's more to self-care than a day at the spa, it can still feel good to treat yourself to some new moisturizer, nail polish, bubble bath or anything else that allows you to pamper yourself. The value is in the intention rather than the product itself. It's not about indulgence; it is simply about taking care of yourself physically and mentally to the best of your ability. You could set yourself a budget – it doesn't have to be much – and choose just one item that will make you feel special. Self-care is all about treating yourself like you matter – you are important, and you do deserve this!

Reflect upon the reasons why you deserve self-care and write them below.

- ....
- ....
- ....
- ....

Create a list of low-budget items that make you feel special.

- ....
- ....
- ....
- ....
- ....

Take a couple of the ideas from above and invest in some me time. In the space below, describe the mental and physical benefits you experienced when taking time for yourself.

....

....

....

....

Staying properly hydrated has numerous benefits, including improving brain function, sleep quality and regulating body temperature. It can be hard to stick to water, but making a conscious effort to stay hydrated can significantly impact your mental and physical well-being.

As an act of self-care, consider different ways to stay hydrated. For example, infusing your water with citrus fruits can make it enjoyable.

Use this space to list different ways of staying hydrated and see what works best for you.

Nobody's perfect, so give yourself credit for everything you're doing right, and be kind to yourself when you struggle.

Lori Deschene

ENJOY MAKING PLANS

We all know that a holiday or day trip can make us feel great, but have you ever thought about the psychological benefits of the planning process? The act of organizing a trip and looking forward to it can make us feel excited and uplifted. The other great news is that a holiday is a gift that keeps on giving. When we talk about it afterwards with friends or look back through our photos, we continue to feel happy and reap the benefits of the experience. The act of going somewhere new can also be a great opportunity to switch off, relax and spend some time prioritizing yourself.

Write a list of places you would like to visit – and they don't have to be big trips abroad. You could include museums or landmarks that interest you.

-
-
-
-
-
-

Choose one of the places from the list above and start to plan your trip. Consider:
- How you are going to get there
- Who, if anyone, will come with you
- How long you will stay
- What else you could do when you are there

Use this space to write your own thoughts.

I WILL NOT LET THE NEGATIVITY OF OTHERS AFFECT ME

Habit Tracker

If you are trying to incorporate several elements of self-care into your daily life, you may find it helpful to make a habit tracker. A habit tracker is simply a chart that includes the habit you would like to adopt, for example "drink more water", and the days of the week. You could use the grid on the opposite page or make your own in your diary or planner to tick off the days when you achieve that element of self-care. This is not only an effective way to hold yourself accountable, but also to celebrate being kind to yourself.

Come up with several different self-care habits you would like to add to your weekly routine and add them to the tracker below. Every time you achieve one of the elements of self-care, give it a tick.

Habits	Mon ✓	Tue ✓	Wed ✓	Thurs ✓	Fri ✓	Sat ✓	Sun ✓

Once the week is complete, reflect upon how incorporating self-care habits into your weekly routine has benefitted you.

Just like the physical act of planting seeds in the soil, there are other meaningful things you can initiate in your life.

Sometimes, we willingly push back on things by starting them on a Monday or the beginning of a new year. Why not start those self-care activities from today?

List things you would like to try today, such as working out for 30 minutes, reading a book for 20 minutes, and so on.

> I'VE BEEN SEARCHING FOR WAYS TO HEAL MYSELF, AND I'VE FOUND THAT KINDNESS IS THE BEST WAY.
>
> Lady Gaga

Slow Cook Something

It can be easy to fall into a pattern of cooking the same food every week. A little variety can be a good thing – both nutritionally and so that meals don't become boring – and if it is cooked with love and patience, so much the better. Why not raid the recipe books or look online for a one-pot, slow cooker recipe for a hearty, comforting meal? If it's something you can prepare in the morning and leave cooking slowly throughout the day, you will be welcomed back to the delicious aroma of home cooking and your dinner waiting. What could be nicer?

The act of cooking can also be a great opportunity to pay attention to your surroundings, helping you to appreciate the smells and textures of the meal you are preparing. Chances are, if you have taken the time to enjoy the process, you will appreciate your meal even more!

Research new meal ideas for breakfast, lunch and dinner. In the space below, write down some of your favourites along with where you found them.

- ....
- ....
- ....
- ....
- ....

Complete the meal planner below. Try to include at least four new recipes throughout the week.

	Breakfast	Lunch	Dinner
Mon			
Tue			
Wed			
Thurs			
Fri			
Sat			
Sun			

Use this space to write your own thoughts.

THE CHALLENGE IS
NOT TO BE PERFECT;
IT'S TO BE WHOLE.

Jane Fonda

FIND YOUR FLOW STATE

You may have heard people talk about finding their "flow state" when they are totally focused on an activity. Although it sounds easy, many of us find it challenging to be truly present when we undertake a task. We can't concentrate or fully enjoy what we are doing because our mind is elsewhere.

Identify something that you could lose yourself in, whether it is a mundane task like doing the washing-up, a more adventurous pursuit like climbing a hill, or a creative activity such as knitting or drawing. Alternatively, you could simply turn your attention to something you had already planned to do and make an effort to be fully present. It could be an afternoon reading a new novel or listening to a podcast without your mind wandering elsewhere. You'll know when you've found that flow state because time will pass without you noticing.

What would you like to achieve by entering your flow state?

Write down any activities you will carry out during your week that you could immerse yourself in.

-
-
-
-

Select one of the activities you identified in the previous prompt and give it your full attention. In the space below, describe how it felt to enter your flow state.

Eating healthy and nutritious foods is a great way to care for yourself. When going grocery shopping, try choosing whole foods such as fruits and vegetables, whole grains (such as oats, brown rice and barley), nuts, beans, fish, shellfish and eggs.

You can even experiment with rainbow food, incorporating a wide variety of fruits and vegetables, all of which offer specific micronutrients, vitamins and minerals. This can make your food wholesome and enjoyable.

Try following healthy eating practices and write down your experience of experimenting with different nutritious foods this week.

....

....

....

....

....

....

....

> BE PRESENT IN ALL THINGS AND THANKFUL FOR ALL THINGS.
>
> Maya Angelou

KNOW YOUR WARNING SIGNS

In order to look after our mental well-being, we need to recognize our own signs of stress and anxiety. These can often present themselves as physical sensations. For example, if someone is saying something that makes you feel vulnerable or unsettled, you might feel a tightening in your chest or throat, or perhaps have a desire to wrap your arms around yourself in protection. Get to know your signs so that you can pause, take a deep breath and then respond with kindness and compassion towards yourself. If you regularly experience physical symptoms of stress or anxiety, seek help from a professional.

Consider times when you have felt stressed or anxious. What physical symptoms have you experienced?

-
-
-
-
-
-

How would you normally react during these times of stress?

Come up with a list of ideas as to how you could respond that would show yourself compassion and kindness.

-
-
-
-
-
-

Use this space to write your own thoughts.

TODAY I CHOOSE SELF-LOVE

Make a Gratitude Jar

It can be easy to take things for granted, so acknowledging the goodness in our lives is a valuable exercise. Studies have shown that gratitude can benefit both your physical and mental health, boosting your mood and flooding your body with feel-good hormones. You could write a daily or weekly gratitude list naming the things you are grateful for, be it health, a favourite TV show, your pet or a close friend. A more fun option could be to start a gratitude jar, finding an empty jar and filling it with scraps of paper detailing all the things that bring you joy. Add to it over time so that when you are feeling blue, you can just grab the jar and reach inside it for a reminder of something good you have in your life.

Imagine this is your gratitude jar. Add anything that brings you joy and that you are grateful for. Why not use your ideas to start a real jar?

Sometimes, you want to shake things up with your friends. You can do that by introducing new activities and exploring different places.

For example, painting and sipping is an interesting activity to participate in. You can get some sheets of paper and coloured pens, and have fun painting with your friends while sipping your favourite drinks.

Use this space to write down other fun things you want to try out with your friends. Maybe a dance workshop?

WHEREVER YOU ARE,
BE THERE TOTALLY.

Eckhart Tolle

SPEND SOME TIME WITH TREES

You might have heard of the term "forest bathing", the Japanese art of relaxing among trees. The idea behind this practice is that simply walking, breathing and being among trees is good for both body and soul.

If this sounds appealing, a trip to the trees could be just what you need. Find a wood, forest or park and spend some time walking around and observing. Breathe deeply and notice the smell of the leaves, or touch the bark. Be curious. How many times have you walked past a tree and failed to take in a single detail about it? See if you can start to recognize different species of trees. Ancient trees are particularly special – there is something awe-inspiring about being in the presence of a living thing that has silently witnessed a hundred years of change.

Take time out for some forest bathing and draw what you observe in the space below. In the leaves, write down as many adjectives that describe the experience as possible.

Use this space to write your own thoughts.

READ A GOOD BOOK

Curling up with a good book must be one of the simplest and most enjoyable pleasures in life. In a world full of demanding technology, reading a physical book can feel like the ultimate indulgence. Why not ask a friend to lend you their latest good read? Or visit a second-hand bookshop or your local library and enjoy the process of browsing and choosing something that sounds enticing? Then, get yourself comfortable and snuggle up!

Consider the genres of books you would like to read and write them below.

-
-
-
-

Research your chosen genres and write a list of books, along with their authors, that you would love to read.

-
-
-
-
-
-
-
-

Next time you reach for the remote, grab a book instead. When you have finished reading it, write a short book review in the space below.

Taking yourself out for a date is a chance to get to know yourself more deeply. Although it can be scary at times because of fear of judgement, it allows you to feel empowered and independent, and is a good form of self-care.

A good idea is to list things you could be scared about when going out on a date with yourself. It will help you face those fears and understand any underlying issues so you can deal with them gradually.

Use this safe space to write down your thoughts about it.

THE WORLD WILL SEE
YOU THE WAY YOU
SEE YOU, AND TREAT
YOU THE WAY YOU
TREAT YOURSELF.

Beyoncé

Candle Meditation

Candle meditation, or candle gazing, is an ancient practice which involves sitting and staring at the flickering flame of a candle. It sounds easy, but in a world where we are more distracted than ever, it can be challenging to sit still. By watching the flame dancing, we can improve our focus and calm the mind.

Find a quiet space and light a candle. Placing it at eye level will stop you from arching your neck. Start by watching the candle for a minute, seeing if you can stay focused. Thoughts will pop up; acknowledge them and allow them to pass as you return your attention to the flame. See if you can gradually build up the duration of your practice over time. How do you feel afterwards?

Use the table below to chart the time you have spent candle gazing during the week. For each meditation, make a note of when you start the exercise and when you finish.

	Mon	Tue	Wed	Thurs	Fri	Sat	Sun
Start time:							
Finish time:							

Using the guidelines below, compose a list of other ways you could incorporate self-care into your life.

Daily (e.g. mindfulness, taking vitamins)
- ....
- ....
- ....
- ....

Weekly (e.g. film night, buying flowers for yourself)
- ....
- ....
- ....
- ....

Monthly (e.g. manicure, reiki)
- ....
- ....
- ....
- ....

Use this space to write your own thoughts.

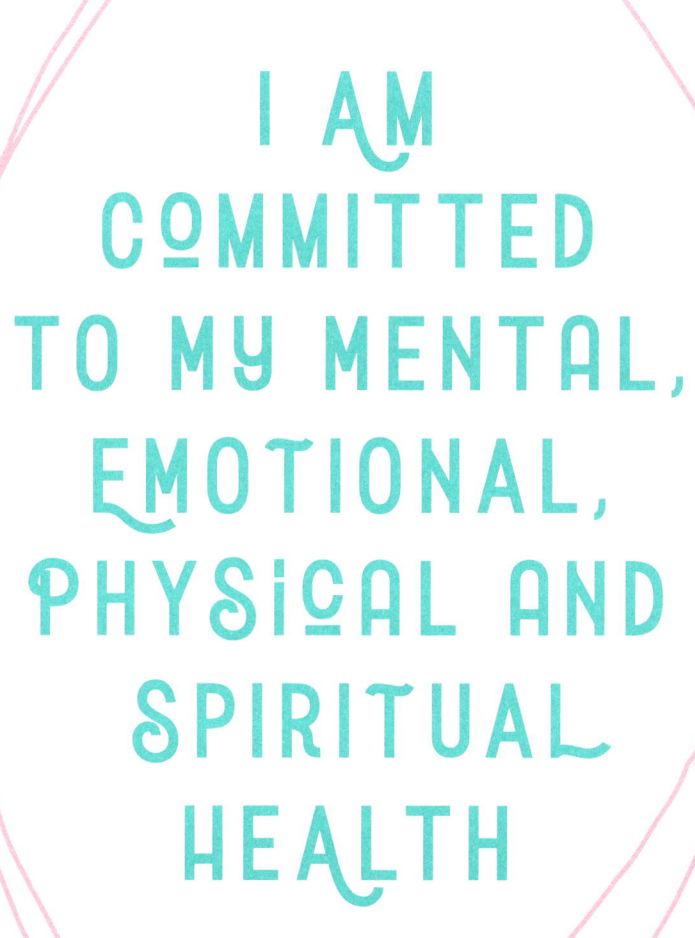

An Hour for You

It can seem hard to make time for the things we love. Work, parenting or life admin can crowd out our passions, and when we do get some time to ourselves, it can be difficult to choose what to do with these precious moments.

Next time you have an hour free, do something that you would love to do. The key to this exercise is to make sure you absolutely do not do what you think you *should* be doing (paying bills, cleaning, answering emails, etc.)! Try to choose something you really want to do. You could paint, write, sleep, practise yoga – whatever it is that you desire. If you feel that inevitable indecision about what to do with your time, try not to put too much pressure on yourself. It's just an hour after all! Go with what might be fun, inspiring or lifts your heart a little.

Write a list of things you enjoy doing that you would love to do more of.

-
-
-
-
-
-

What holds you back from doing things you would like to do?

In the space below, come up with solutions that could help you find more time to do what you love. For example, micro-tidying could help you carve out more time while still making your home a haven.

Have you ever been curious about learning a new skill? Studies show that learning new skills helps thicken the prefrontal cortex and makes you feel more empowered.

For example, you can take a beginner's workshop on coffee making and learn how to use different techniques to become a barista yourself.

Use this space to write down different skills you'd like to try to learn.

SURROUND YOURSELF
WITH PEOPLE AND
THINGS THAT
INSPIRE YOU.
LEARN EVERYTHING
YOU CAN.

Jameela Jamil

Make a Bedtime Routine

Many people have a set morning routine, whether that includes early workouts, mindfulness practices, making a smoothie or planning the day ahead. A good morning regime can set you up for the day ahead. It also sets a precedent for your day and how it will look and feel. But have you considered planning a bedtime routine?

Winding down effectively and preparing yourself for rest could help you sleep better. There are plenty of activities you could include: perhaps a few minutes of yoga, writing in a gratitude journal, spritzing an aromatherapy sleep spray onto your pillows or a quick tidy of your bedside table. Try to avoid looking at any devices that emit blue light because this can negatively affect levels of the sleep-inducing hormone melatonin. Just taking a few little steps like this can get your body ready for sleep and give you the gift of a peaceful and rejuvenating slumber.

Create a bedtime routine to encourage a restful night's sleep. Find activities that make you feel relaxed and peaceful. Try putting this routine into practice for a week. Every time you complete an element of the routine, give it a tick.

	M	T	W	TH	F	SA	SU
	☐	☐	☐	☐	☐	☐	☐
	☐	☐	☐	☐	☐	☐	☐
	☐	☐	☐	☐	☐	☐	☐
	☐	☐	☐	☐	☐	☐	☐
	☐	☐	☐	☐	☐	☐	☐
	☐	☐	☐	☐	☐	☐	☐
	☐	☐	☐	☐	☐	☐	☐

When the week is complete, document how having a calming bedtime routine benefitted your sleep in the space below.

Use this space to write your own thoughts.

> HONESTLY, SELF-CARE IS NOT FLUFFY — IT'S SOMETHING WE SHOULD TAKE SERIOUSLY.
>
> Kris Carr

Final Word

While the term "self-care" may sound self-indulgent, this is not the case. This practice is simply nourishing your emotional and physical well-being, and in a world that seems constantly on the go, taking time out to concentrate on yourself is an essential part of life. Self-care is not simply about pampering; it can take any number of forms, from deciding to treat yourself to a warm drink, to spending an afternoon watching an old movie in your comfiest pyjamas.

Let go of that guilt and spend some time tending to your own needs. The moment you start to feel overwhelmed or anxious, come back to this journal to remind yourself of ways you can put your well-being first. Give yourself permission to prioritize yourself – even if it's only for a few minutes a day. After all, you deserve it.

Mindfulness for Every Day Journal

Simple Tips and Guided Exercises to Help You Live in the Moment

Paperback

ISBN: 978-1-80007-835-2

Positivity for Every Day Journal

Simple Tips and Guided Exercises to Help You Look on the Bright Side

Paperback

ISBN: 978-1-80007-833-8

Resilience for Every Day Journal

Simple Tips and Guided Exercises to Help You Find Your Inner Strength

Paperback

ISBN: 978-1-80007-834-5

Happiness for Every Day Journal

Simple Tips and Guided Exercises to Help You Find Joy

Paperback

ISBN: 978-1-80007-832-1

Have you enjoyed this book? If so, find us on Facebook at **Summersdale Publishers**, on Twitter at **@Summersdale** and on Instagram, TikTok and Bluesky at **@summersdalebooks** and get in touch. We'd love to hear from you!

www.summersdale.com

Image Credits

Design elements throughout © Nadya_Art/Shutterstock.com, p.11 – flowers © Singleline/Shutterstock.com; p.31 – icon © pking4th/Shutterstock.com; p.51 – pins © Realstockvector/Shutterstock.com; p.55 – suns © IIIerlok_xolms/Shutterstock.com, clouds © Oleh Svetiukha/Shutterstock.com; p.59 – droplet © Haali/Shutterstock.com; p.95 – twinkles © ysclips design/Shutterstock.com; p.135 – jar © Chereliss/Shutterstock.com; p.139 – leaves © VikiVector/Shutterstock.com